Disclaimer: All ideas suggested in this book may include a certain amount of risk. The publisher and author disclaim any responsibility and any liability for any injury, harm, or illness that may occur through or by use of any information in this book.

ISBN: 978-0-9847801-0-5
ISBN: 0984780106

To buy books in quantity or schedule a speaking engagement, contact us at
Bulk purchases: sales@ICanFixAmerica.com
Speaking engagements: speaking@ICanFixAmerica.com
Online store and website: www.ICanFixAmerica.com
Facebook: I Can Fix America
Twitter: @ICanFixAmerca
Because we practice what we preach: Book printed in the United States of America
Printed on 30% recycled paper with environmentally friendly soy-blend ink

Paper for coverstock is 100% recycled, pigments and sealants are 90% water-based, corrugated shipping containers are 80% recycled material, kraft paper is used instead of Styrofoam for packing, none of the adhesives contain lead or phthalates, the hot melt adhesives are free of volatile organic compounds (VOC) and the water based adhesives contain less than 0.4% VOC.

MADE IN THE USA

"There is NO LIMIT TO WHAT A MAN CAN DO OR HOW FAR HE CAN GO if he doesn't mind who gets the credit."

— ROBERT WOODRUFF

DEDICATION & THANKS

There are so many people, so many events and so many life experiences that have been woven together to create this book. I know I will forget some, but I first want to send a special thank you to the people who have made this book and turned my crazy ideas into reality:

Rosie Falconi for the magic you possess by taking my barely legible scribbles and turning them into wonderful illustrations that tell a story often better than words. If it weren't for you, your talents and love this book wouldn't be nearly what it is today. This is the beginning of our journey together and I look forward to great things with you at my side for the rest of my life.

Nicki Schroeder for your talent and vision reflected in the beautiful layout, design and usability of this book.

Holly Roseberry for your comprehensive edits (I knew I should have paid more attention in English class), snarky comments and holding me and the purpose of this book to the highest standards.

And most importantly, I want to thank the following people who believed and supported me all my life, through the good times and bad, and who made me want to be the best I could be at whatever I put my mind to:

To all my Emory University and Oxford College friends and family who taught me to think and see the world with a different set of eyes. Bill Fox, for some reason you believed (almost immediately) that this young kid from Flint, Michigan, was worthy of your love, wisdom and generosity. You've supported me in everything I've set my mind to inside and outside of college. You have made me a better person. Steve Walton, you too have always been a great friend and supporter, but most valued, a "challenger" of my ideas. Thank you for always being there.

To my Vistage CEO family who is always there to make me stronger, wiser, more responsible and simply a better human being and steward of the enormous gifts and blessings that have been bestowed and entrusted to me.

To Bill Schwarz who has taught me to see the world in truer, clearer ways by putting my ego in check and constantly challenging the higher purpose of design, whether it be in my companies or in my life.

My late Uncle Hick who taught me that the greatest among us are those who serve his fellow man. I have yet to meet anyone who served his family, friends, country and community greater than you did through your 93 years of life. If I can be half the man that you were, my life will be a success.

My brother Jon and sister Linda who have always been there to support me, annoy me, challenge me and put me in my place. I love you both.

My Aunt Sherron and Uncle Jack who, for as long as I can remember, have been my second set of parents. Especially after Dad died, you guys stepped up and were there for me, Jon and Mom, making sure we could make the baseball practices, the after-school meetings and the dentist appointments.

To my late father Lee who died when I was 14 years old. You taught me the value of work, the importance of character and the solemn respect for doing what you say you are going to do. You didn't believe in allowance because you said that wasn't how the real world worked. I never understood, until I was much older, how wise your words were. You provided everything I ever needed and wanted … the magic was you made me work for things that I valued the most. Dad, I have lived my life knowing that if I want something of value, I'm going to have to work for it and that it is squarely up to me to make things happen. I know that you would be proud of this book and the man I have become.

And finally, to my mother Susan. You have been the one who has always trusted me, believed in me, supported me in every way and also gave me enough space to allow me to learn one of the greatest gifts in the world … that when you fail, all that matters is that you get up and move forward. You allowed and encouraged me to do anything I wanted knowing full well that the chance of failure was always there. Whenever I did fail, you reassured me and the person who I am to strive for the next great thing. You are the most generous and loving person I know. You taught me to see love and goodness in everything. If it weren't for your struggle and the sacrifice you made to make sure I had the best chance to succeed, to learn and to grow I wouldn't be the person I am today. I love you and dedicate this book to you.

USE THIS BOOK!

There are a few ways you can read this book. You can go traditional and start at the beginning. Thumb through the illustrations and stop at something that catches your eye. Or check out the list of macro issues below and start with what concerns you the most. The issues you will be fixing:

STABILIZE HOUSING
#1 & #29

BE GOOD STEWARDS OF OUR MONEY AND RESOURCES
#2, #13, #33 & #38

RESPECT OUR ELDERS AND LEARN FROM HISTORY
#3 & #39

STOP ENTITLEMENT THINKING
#4, #34, #45 & #51

BUILD UP EDUCATION
#5, #14 & #35

HELP SOLVE UNEMPLOYMENT
#6, #8 & #43

BECOME SELF-RELIANT

#7, #10, #16, #21 & #42

FIX GOVERNMENT AND ITS ROLE IN OUR LIVES

#9, #27, #41 & #49

DEFINE YOUR PRINCIPLES AND LIVE BY THEM

#11, #25, #40 & #47

FOCUS ON UNITY, NOT DIVERSITY

#12, #22, #37, #44, #48 & #52

CURE OURSELVES AND OUR HEALTHCARE SYSTEM

#15, #20, #28, #36, #46 & #50

BE OPEN AND CONTINUE TO LEARN

#17 & #30

GIVE GENEROUSLY

#18, #24, #26 & #32

CREATE COMMUNITY AND ACCOUNTABILITY

#19, #23 & #31

AND SO HERE WE ARE...

"Damn you math teachers" was a constant, internal chant that seemed to permeate my soul whenever I found out I had to take a math class. Starting in grade school all the way through college I never really was a fan of the subject. Sure, I understood the basics but why in the world would I need to know about angles, calculus, probabilities and statistics? We have all had the conversation amongst ourselves: "Will I ever use this stuff in the real world?"

However, there are basic math principles that when embraced actually become magical. They can tell the future and help predict outcomes. They can strike fear and keep people up at night. These basic principles take no sides and speak only the truth. And no matter how they are "spun" you cannot violate them and expect a different result. For example, no matter how hard I try to convince myself that 10 - 9 = 0, I would be wrong. I would be wrong any way that I tried to rationalize the last equation as truth, as a sustainable principle. Sure, if I was in the right position I might be able to run a campaign or instruct my legion of workers to believe our new company slogan, you know, that 10 - 9 = 0. But even though I heard it over and over again there probably would be something in my gut telling me that this wasn't right.

In America today, I fear that we have lost the truth of principles that are as enduring as basic math, truths about the economy, business, the role of government, how to be healthy and how to build a prosperous future. At almost every turn we have violated simple, historically proven principles. A few simple examples:

We have violated the financial principle that we cannot spend more money than we make and expect to be prosperous, both in our individual lives and in government at every level.

We have violated the laws of health by assuming that we can eat whatever we want and exercise as little as we want without suffering the short- and long-term consequences.

And above all else we have violated, in my opinion, the most important principle of all: That one person can make a difference and that we are not all the same. Instead, we have created a society where everyone gets a trophy and mediocrity is accepted and oftentimes rewarded. While it is true that the Declaration of Independence says that all men are created equal, it is not true that all men possess the same abilities, talents and opportunities.

It is important for us to realize what our talents are and use them for the highest purpose possible, strive for excellence, and not squander the gifts that have been given to us.

Over the past 50 years or so we have increasingly looked to government to solve many of the social and economic problems that we have faced. We have effectively "outsourced" many of these problems to an entity that, by design, cannot solve or effectively manage these problems. The government wasn't designed to create jobs. The government wasn't designed to provide people who don't have health care to be given health care, and, above all else, the government wasn't designed to be our personal nanny to make sure that everything we do and everywhere we go has limited risk associated with it.

It is funny to me that as I look back on my own life, from my first 18 years of growing up in Flint, Michigan, through my last 18 years of going to college and working in the greater Atlanta area, that I attributed so much of what happened as "outside of my control." I justified one business failure as a victim of the dot-com crash, and reasoned that another one of my businesses wasn't able to reach its potential because of the recent housing collapse. For a while there, I guess I had a victim mentality or a case of the "blame-o's" (new word I just created). Early on in my life I really had nothing but success in almost anything I set my mind to, and it was important to me (at the time) to go through the checklist to make sure I was truly living life … you know, the really important stuff like going to homecoming with the homecoming queen, being elected high school class president, getting into a good school, being elected president of the undergraduate college, trying to date hot chicks, driving a fancy car, etc. (Arrogant, right?)

My friends ask me why in the world would I write this book? The answer is simple: To me, America is on a path in which we will soon lose the magic that propelled this country to greatness in less than 200 years (a short time in world history).

I believe this magic had a lot to do with being good neighbors and good stewards of finances and our vast natural resources, but above all the "hunger" that many Americans had to make their life better through hard work, innovation and a sense of community. The simple truth of an America "not too long ago" is that if you didn't work, if you didn't contribute, you didn't get paid. And if you didn't get paid you (and maybe your family) actually did go hungry … there was no fallback plan other than the generosity of the people in your community to help if you had tried your best but failed. The difference I see in America today is that we are almost running on empty with the old "I will give it the best I can" work ethic. Today, there are multiple scenarios in which people get compensated by the government to be unemployed. In my opinion, there is only one time in people's life in which they should be paid to be unemployed. That's called retirement. Sure, I understand that times are tough and that there isn't a perfect job out there for everybody. The tough facts are that people might have to do things that they normally would not like to do, including: educate themselves on a new set of skills; take a tough, manual labor job; join the military to protect our country; or, above all else, start a small business doing something, whether it be cooking, cleaning, painting, yard work, anything.

Motivated by the spirit that simple math (not the "fuzzy" math that Wall Street or the "fantasy" math that government uses) does not tell a lie, I felt compelled to write this book. Is it a math book? Nope. But it is a book that will attempt to frame many of the large "macro" issues facing America and distill them down to tasks that the majority of us can do in our own daily lives. Applying the mathematical principles of probability, if enough of us actually get off our butts and start doing these things, the odds increase that our country will move in a positive direction.

We are, I believe, at a tipping point in American society and history. We can no longer wait for the economy to pick back up in order to get to work. We can no longer believe that by voting a certain way on a certain date, we will miraculously end up on Recovery Road. It is somewhat tantamount to saying that you are in peak physical shape right after the first time you run around the block, which we all know is wrong, regardless of how much we try to convince ourselves otherwise.

Today, right now, we have to stop the destructive things we are doing, in each of our lives, and consciously decide to make America great again. Instead of blaming other people, look inside this book and find something, anything, that you can do better in your life. Each effort counts and moves us closer in reclaiming and ultimately preserving the greatest country and way of life the world has ever known.

But before you get to work, I want to apologize first. I, personally, have let you down. I didn't buy American when I should have bought American. I didn't think through all the consequences of spending money on materialistic crap I didn't need instead of helping out a person truly in need. I invested money in the stock market in the hopes that I would "catch a wave" of stock price increase and appreciation, all the time knowing that this thing I called "investing in stocks" was really just legalized gambling. And above all, for a while there, I just stood on the sidelines and thought that if I just kept my head down and worked, our leaders would make sure the country stayed on the right path. I sort of outsourced my responsibilities both as a citizen and as a steward of the blessing given to all of us called the American Dream to politicians and companies that were not aligned with my and America's best interests.

Well, I'm not going to let that happen again.

Today, I am going to commit to being better. Inside this book are 52 simple ideas and action items that almost anyone can do to make real change in our personal lives and the lives of our fellow Americans. Sure, the whole world needs help, but unless we get our own house in order how can we truly serve our neighbors? A strong and sustainable America makes the whole world a better place. But we have work, tough work, to do to regain our strength and create a sustainable economy.

So let's get to work. I am not waiting for you, but I want you to join me. None of us can wait for the other. We need to start now with the things we can do better, the better choices we can make today to ensure a strong America tomorrow.

I Can Fix America.

Who's with me?

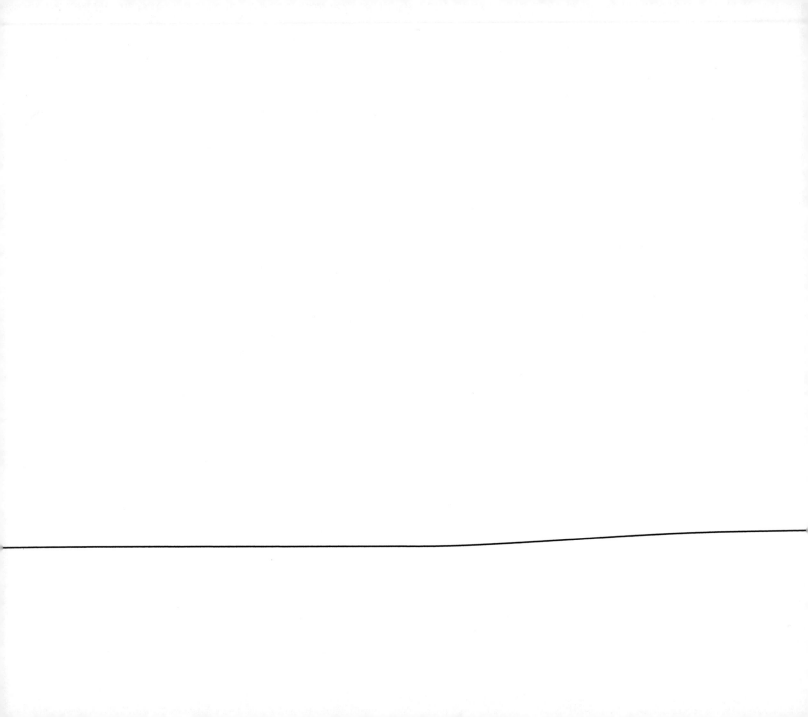

I CAN

FIX AMERICA

52 common sense ways YOU can make the United States great again.

A book by David Duley
Illustrated by Rosie Falconi

I Can Media, LLC.
Atlanta, Georgia

#1 ———————————————————

I CAN

MOW THE YARD OR HELP MAINTAIN A FORECLOSURE in my neighborhood should I notice that it has gotten unsightly.

More curb appeal = potentially more value when house is sold = less negative impact on the value of your home.

Sure, smaller banks might not be as "convenient" as big banks. But what we trade for convenience often leaves us powerless once a crisis happens. I'd rather try to sort things out with a local bank than constantly get the runaround with larger institutions.

I CAN

MOVE MY FINANCIAL ACCOUNTS

to a smaller local bank or credit union to shift the power away from the mega banks and promote the value of personal relationships in the industry.

#3

I CAN

CALL OR VISIT THE MOST SIGNIFICANT ELDER IN MY LIFE,

learn about his life and thank him for what he contributed to our world. By listening, documenting and sharing his story I Can keep his legacy alive.

He might not have an email account but chances are he knows a heck of a lot more about service and sacrifice than you do. Sorry to break the news to ya but you're not that unique. Our elders have lived through hard times and there is much we can learn that applies to what is going on today.

Nobody is perfect. Few people really want to cause harm to other people. Accidents happen and that's just part of life. Unfortunately, lawyers were invented and have abused many people, companies and communities in the pursuit of money. If you have been wronged, at least give negotiating a chance before you call 1-800-LAWYER.

I CAN

accept that mistakes and accidents do happen and choose **NOT TO RUSH TO SUE PEOPLE,** should I become a victim of an incident beyond their reasonable control.

I CAN

FORM A "SCHOLARSHIP CLUB"
WITH MY NEIGHBORS AND FRIENDS

to help support the college education of someone who
would not be able to attend college without our help.

The only real long-term investment that will yield massive returns is an educated citizenry. Other countries are kicking our butt and our government has been less than stellar in making our students competitive and knowledgeable in the workplace. Find and invest in a promising child if you want to leave a legacy.

Umm...when was the last time you went to a career fair? Good times, huh? I doubt it. If you are making money through some set of skills you've developed, try to find someone who is unemployed who you can teach those skills to. Government isn't going to do it, and neither are companies that aren't hiring or hiring for a certain skill set.

I CAN

mentor someone who is unemployed with the hopes

that through my sharing and guidance **I WILL**

PROVIDE ENOUGH KNOWLEDGE AND SKILLS SO THAT SHE CAN BECOME EMPLOYABLE.

I CAN

DOWNSIZE MY LIFE IF I AM STRESSED OUT ABOUT MONEY AND STRUGGLING TO PAY THE BILLS. I Can create a budget to live within my means, sell the fancy car or boat, and make purchasing decisions based on what I need, not what I want. I Can achieve financial peace of mind.

If you have enough money for a big, flat-screen TV, a boat or a new car yet somehow can't pay the rent or your mortgage then your priorities are out of whack. Sell the materialistic crap and focus on what really matters.

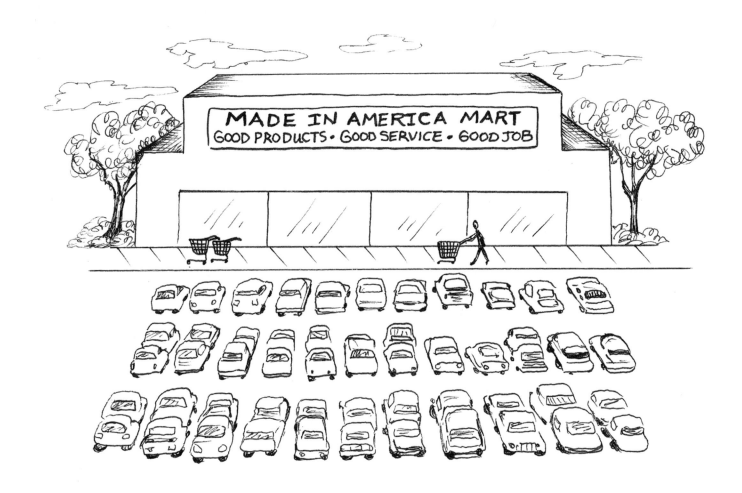

I know you can't buy certain things that are made in America anymore, but for those items that are made in America (cars, furniture, appliances), make a conscious decision to buy American. If enough people do, then other items will come back to America (clothing, electronics, everything else). If you don't, please do not complain that you are unemployed.

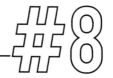

I CAN

BUY MORE GOODS AND SERVICES THAT ARE MADE IN AMERICA,

from companies that are headquartered in America,
if I truly want more American jobs created.

#9

I CAN

SUPPORT TAX REFORM THAT ALLOWS AMERICANS TO TAKE HOME MORE OF THEIR $$ in the hopes that it will be used to support charities and others who are truly in need.

There is a great saying, "For whom much is given, much is expected." If it comes to pass that America can reform its antiquated tax system and you benefit from that, then do the right thing and help those in need. It is not the government's responsibility... it is yours. Unless, of course, you want to pay higher taxes.

One of the few, tangible things listed in the Bill of Rights is our right to bear arms. If you choose to own a gun, make sure you know how to use it safely. It is fantasy to believe that a world can exist without guns. Because the criminals have guns (and will always have guns), it is probably a good idea for you to be armed too.

I CAN

SAFELY AND LEGALLY LEARN HOW TO HANDLE AND STORE A GUN

in order to protect my property and family
from harm or assault.

#11

I CAN

find courage to **STAND UP FOR WHAT I BELIEVE** even though it might make me uncomfortable and vulnerable to criticism. I Can live my life grounded in my principles and use them as my anchor in a turbulent world.

I read a great quote (widely attributed to Howard Cosell) a while back: "What's right isn't always popular. What's popular isn't always right." Now, more than ever, America needs true leaders grounded in the common good willing to serve the common man. It's about action, not just words.

Without the unimaginable sacrifice numerous men and women make each year to serve our country in the armed services nothing else would matter. These people are the true heroes and role models. Whenever you can, help them out, thank them and shake their hand.

I CAN

SHOW MY GRATITUDE TO MEMBERS OF THE MILITARY BY THANKING THEM

and shaking their hand, or anonymously buying

a meal or a drink the next time I see one in a restaurant.

#13

I CAN

assess my lifestyle and my family's needs to **FIND WAYS FOR US TO LIVE MORE ENERGY EFFICIENTLY** in order to help America become energy independent.

Face it, if we were energy independent we really wouldn't be fighting wars in the Middle East now, would we? Becoming energy independent might be the greatest job creator and national security policy we could ever implement. Do your part to make it happen.

We cannot wait on the government, unions and administrators to fix the school system. We need to roll up our sleeves and make it happen ourselves. Support the teachers and make sure they know that you will provide time or money if they need it.

I CAN

ask a public school principal if I CAN "ADOPT" A TEACHER to make sure he has the necessary resources to do his job so the youth of America will excel. If the principal denies this request, I Can do it anyway.

#15

I CAN

COMMIT THIS MONTH TO EXERCISING,
with the goal that it will become a lifetime commitment.

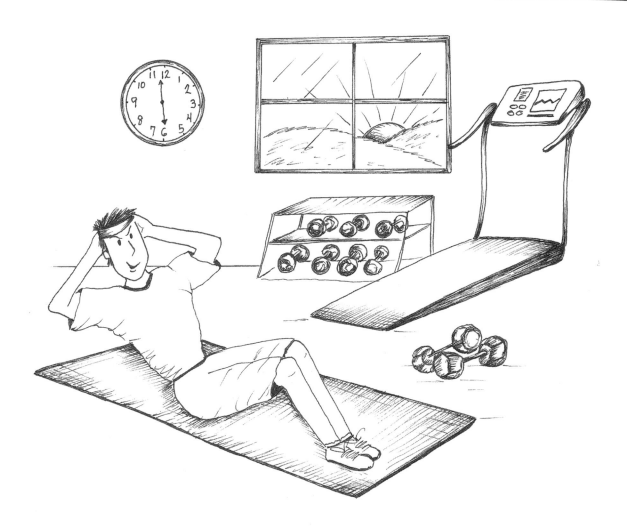

Rocky did not fight and eventually beat Ivan Drago in *Rocky IV* by sitting around watching TV. No, he split wood, dragged a sleigh through snow, ran up a mountain and then did triceps curls with a bag of rocks on a pulley. The better you feel physically, the better you will perform. And we need a lot of high performers to get America back on track.

You are not a weirdo if you hope for the best but plan for the worst. You are just plain smart and prudent. Make sure you help not only yourself and family but also are of service to others.

I CAN

CREATE A DISASTER PLAN FOR MY FAMILY AND ME in case something terrible happens on either a global scale (terrorism) or local scale (tornado). I Can plan on helping others in need in either case.

#17

I CAN

visit a church or other house of worship with a set of beliefs different from my own in order to understand my fellow Americans better and PUT TO REST ANY MISUNDERSTANDINGS I HAVE ABOUT OTHER RELIGIONS.

We are a nation built on freedom. That freedom allows for any belief system out there, even if it doesn't jibe with your own. Respect each other and the great freedom we have and don't do anything stupid to jeopardize it.

Striving for financial success and independence is what founded and built America. Hard work and innovation should be rewarded and you should be able to relish in it. Just don't be a jerk. Give generously to those who truly need it and invest in other people who want to create innovative and socially important projects.

I CAN

accept that it is OK to strive for financial success and that it is

OK to be rich as long as **I GIVE GENEROUSLY TO THOSE LESS FORTUNATE** and make the world

a better place through my own good fortune.

I CAN

VOTE IN EVERY ELECTION. Prior to voting I Can commit to being educated about the candidates and issues to ensure that I am judging them based on the content of their character and intentions.

Do your homework to learn about the candidates and how their position affects the long-term viability of America. Quit voting out of your own self-interest and short-term gains. We have serious problems and we need serious problem solvers, not more game show hosts.

While the thought of Twinkies might bring back that lovin' feeling, also know that it will most likely send you to the grave early. Our bodies are designed for natural food. Nobody has a perfect diet, but we can do better.

20

I CAN

reduce my risk of cancer, stroke, diabetes and obesity by

EATING LESS PROCESSED FOOD

and more fruits, vegetables and lean meats.

#21

I CAN

PUT TOGETHER A REALISTIC FINANCIAL PLAN that doesn't rely on any government assistance in the form of Social Security or health care. Should those programs exist when I retire, I Can use them to add to my income, choices and peace of mind.

Live today with tomorrow in mind. Make a plan today that will allow you to become financially independent as soon as possible. For many of us, that means planning for retirement. However, be aware that if you don't do the tough work today you will mostly likely have zero retirement in the future. That means you will work as a greeter until you drop dead. Think about it.

Simply put: If it wasn't for these brave men and women you would be speaking German, Japanese, maybe even French. But you're not; you're speaking English. (Well, most of you, anyway.) You know why? Because when the crap hit the fan these people went out and put their lives on the line so you could continue living yours. They are the best of America and need to be treated accordingly.

22

I CAN

ADOPT A MILITARY FAMILY while their loved one is deployed and make sure they have the resources and support to make it through the difficult times.

#23

I CAN

CHECK THE FACTS before I pass on information or rumors that I hear.

Seriously, don't be a gossiper. No one respects them and these people pretty much suck. This viewpoint has stood the test of time.

If you have worked hard enough to be in a leadership role within a company, treat your people well. Low wages for start-up companies, nonprofits and companies that have yet to turn a profit is understandable. However, if you are rolling in the dough, acknowledge that you didn't get there by yourself and share your prosperity with those who helped you along the way.,

I CAN

PAY LIVING WAGES to people that I manage or employ should they work for me on a full-time basis.

I CAN

decide whether I value a world where personal freedom is sacrificed for the sake of security, or a world where security is sacrificed for the sake of personal freedom. I Can be ready to STAND UP FOR THE PATH THAT I THINK IS BEST.

Who do you want controlling your security and destiny? You or the government? With liberty comes responsibility. Be a good steward of liberty.

Some people in the service industry are bad. Some are good. And then some are really good. Award great service when you experience it. This is wealth redistribution we can all believe in!

26

I CAN

LEAVE AN OUTRAGEOUS TIP the next time I receive excellent service from someone in the hospitality or service industry.

I CAN

WRITE LOCAL AND NATIONAL POLITICIANS

and urge them to pass balanced budget amendments.

It would be nice to believe that those in elected office can be financially responsible. Unfortunately, that is not their track record. Therefore, to limit the damage these people can continue to do we must rein in their ability to spend money. Their allowance is cut off until further notice. Sorry.

Now doctors don't know everything, even though sometimes they act like they do. Chances are, however, that they know more than you about how to be healthy. Listen to them and take their recommendations seriously.

I CAN

ASK MY DOCTOR HOW I CAN BE HEALTHIER and then

follow that recommendation.

I CAN

BUY A FORECLOSED HOME to help stabilize

the housing crisis and provide a family with an affordable and nice home in which to live. I Can also enhance my personal cash flow and net worth when I purchase this property at a discounted price.

Ben Rothschild, of English nobility and banking, is credited with saying, "The time to buy is when there's blood in the streets." I don't think he meant literal blood but I know some parts of town where you might find some. The truth is this: If you can buy a solid house for what it sold for 40 years ago chances are you are getting a good deal. If in the next 10 years the house is worthless, then we are all screwed – the whole nation – and it won't matter one bit.

"I don't have enough time to learn a new language, I don't have time to learn a new skill, I don't have time to figure out how this computer thing works." Stop watching TV and wasting time online and voilà ... time appears.

30

I CAN

CUT BACK ON WATCHING TV AND SURFING THE WEB by one hour per week and spend that time reading about topics and ideas that I always wanted to understand.

#31

I CAN

BE A RESPONSIBLE AND ACTIVE PARENT.

I Can play a key role in the financial, educational and social development of any child I have created and honor all responsibilities to give my child the best chance to succeed and become a productive member of society.

Practicing making babies is fun. Changing diapers and paying for all sorts of expenses is not so fun. Be smart and be accountable for your actions because they do have consequences. If you bring a life into this world accept the responsibility and be a good parent. It is the most important responsibility you have on Earth and your character and life will be judged on your action or inaction.

It's easy to give a homeless person money while you pass them by. It's hard to figure out a way to make sure that person isn't homeless anymore. As an old saying goes, "Give a man a fish and he will eat for a day. Teach a man to fish and he will eat for a lifetime."

32

I CAN

TALK TO A HOMELESS PERSON for five minutes to see how, other than giving cash, I Can help this person get back on her feet and find stability.

#33

I CAN

write and encourage business and political leaders to make America entirely energy independent **BY MANAGING THE FOSSIL FUELS WITHIN THE BORDERS OF AMERICA** while capitalizing on the promise of renewable energy.

Oil is not evil; we've just been getting it from the wrong people. Likewise, solar, wind, nuclear and natural gas are all viable solutions and extremely abundant. This is not a difficult question or a complex answer. The solution is all of the above and we need to promote ways to become truly energy independent if America is to survive.

Under almost every circumstance we have the ability to become successful entrepreneurs. If you are unhappy about your income or job, start a small business. You don't have to quit your job to do this. You will just have to work harder than you've ever worked before and take risks. Tough, but as we know, life isn't easy. It often rewards the risk takers.

34

I CAN

START A SMALL BUSINESS full time or
on the side if I am unhappy with my current income or job.

#35

I CAN

find a promising child who lives in a struggling part of town and
PROVIDE HIM WITH THE RESOURCES
to go to a summer camp, further his education, and remove him from potentially bad situations within the neighborhood.

Some of us were born into families that are financially better off than others. Thus, we are often born into better neighborhoods, schools and circles of friends. There are huge parts of town that have been suffering through gang-related and other societal problems. If you live near those neighborhoods, go find promising young adults and get them out of temptation to get into trouble during the summer months. You could literally save a life.

If we could get our own personal health in order then huge change would happen seemingly overnight within health care. In fact, there was a recent study* which stated if we could just make better decisions about staying a healthy weight and eating well and stopped smoking we could potentially save $1,000,000,000,000 a year in direct and indirect costs. Yes, that is what 1 trillion dollars looks like. Health care fixed. Done.

Milken Institute: An Unhealthy America, October 2007

I CAN

LOSE WEIGHT IF I AM OVERWEIGHT AND/OR QUIT SMOKING if I smoke,

knowing that this will not only benefit me and the ones who love me but also help reduce healthcare expenses throughout America.

I CAN

TELL SOMEONE HOW GRATEFUL I AM TO BE AN AMERICAN and express to that person how I am getting involved to make sure America remains the world's best place to live.

It is OK to be a proud American. No country is perfect, but I would argue that while we certainly have faults, no nation on Earth is more generous with time and treasure than Americans. If you are embarrassed by America you have two choices: 1) Work to fix, through action not just words, the issues you think are wrong; or 2) Feel free to move to one of the other 195 countries in the world. Choose one and get busy.

By recycling and buying products packaged and made with recycled materials you Can help save the planet and create jobs. It has been estimated that recycling, reuse and composting create six to 10 times as many jobs as waste incineration and landfills. – *Clean Air Campaign*

I CAN

ask companies from which I buy goods and services to
BE ENVIRONMENTALLY CONSCIOUS IN THEIR BUSINESS PRACTICES AND PACKAGING.

#39

I CAN

URGE MY CONGRESSPERSON TO ADHERE TO TIME-TESTED PRINCIPLES OF FREE MARKET CAPITALISM in which people are rewarded for taking risks to build innovative, job-creating companies that keep America's high standard of living sustainable. I Can share my conviction that we cannot bail out or subsidize any business and expect the long-term outcome to be positive or fair.

The reason we haven't re-created the wheel is because the wheel works. For some reason, these people we elect to office like to make the same mistakes year after year. It is insanity. Despite all the chatter you hear about how complicated issues are, they really aren't too hard to solve. What is difficult are the tough, unpopular decisions that have to be made today to pay for the poor decisions of the past.

It's easy to play the victim card. Sometimes it's even comforting. But to really move forward in life we must leave the past behind. What's done is done and the only thing we can control, from this point forward, is the future. Focus on doing the tough things that lead to success and soon you will find it.

I CAN

dig deep within myself and find something or someone for whom I harbor resentment. **I CAN FORGIVE, LET IT GO, AND NEVER USE IT AGAIN AS AN EXCUSE FOR ANYTHING.**

#41

I CAN

encourage lawmakers to obey the rule of law and to
ADDRESS IMMIGRATION REFORM
in order to speed up the process of getting productive
citizens into the workforce and contributing to the tax base.

Unless you are a Native American, chances are someone in your family was an immigrant. Not enforcing our immigration laws has created our immigration problem. Now that the horse is out of the barn let's figure out a way to get good, otherwise law-abiding, hardworking people into the taxpaying system and on a path to citizenship. If you want to solve some real problems, how about moving illegal immigrants and other non-citizens up to the front of the line for citizenship if they buy foreclosed homes. Hmmmmm...

If you have carried a balance on your credit card the past year then you need to commit to using it only for absolute emergencies (someone dies/emergency health issue). Don't buy anything on your credit card unless you pay it off each month. If you can't afford to pay cash for it, don't buy it.

I CAN

COMMIT TO LIVE MY LIFE WITHOUT CREDIT CARD DEBT.

#43

I CAN

COMMIT TO SUPPORT A LOCAL SMALL BUSINESS that I have not tried before at least once a month.

If you want to truly bring accountability, jobs and customer service back into your life then support local small businesses. Without them, we run the risk of being able to do business only with mega corporations that often lack customer service and community accountability.

It is 100 percent your right to believe in and worship God any way you see fit. You can also choose not to believe in religion or God...that's OK too. But don't use your religion or beliefs to judge, discriminate against or belittle other people. Live your life through love, service and respect and everything will work out.

I CAN

accept that it is OK to **STRIVE FOR A STRONG RELATIONSHIP WITH A HIGHER POWER** and live my life according to those beliefs so long as I do not judge or cause harm to others.

#45

I CAN

MAKE SURE THAT IF I BELONG TO A UNION, THE LEADERSHIP AND MEMBERS ARE DOING WHAT IS BEST FOR ALL INVOLVED.

If I am a member of a teachers union, I Can make sure the students' interest and success are put first. If I am a member of a business union, I Can make sure that contracts are negotiated to provide common sense business principles without a sense of entitlement. And finally, if I am a member of a government union, I Can make sure we are doing what is best and most efficient for the delivery of services to the citizens and taxpayers of America.

Unions, you have a place at the table of commerce but make sure that you don't ruin the meal by making unreasonable demands based on the rules and structure of the past. The world's economy has drastically changed and you need to change with it. You have done great things for the workers of America. Keep fighting but be reasonable.

As we get older, we get a little more complacent. Things don't fire us up like they used to. Part of the problem is we lose some of our competitive spirit. Enter a competition and get your butt kicked by someone twice your age. That will help motivate ya.

I CAN

COMMIT TO ENTER A COMPETITION

in order to gain a greater sense of discipline and a competitive spirit.

I CAN

STAY COMMITTED AND BEHAVE ACCORDINGLY

when I am in committed relationships.

Seriously, if you are committed to someone then respect that person and behave the way you would like him or her to behave. If you think you've made a mistake or are unable to live up to your commitments then discuss this with your partner and make a plan. Maybe your partner feels the same way.

The respect we need to have for these people can be summed up by the following statement: While you are running away from danger, these people are running into it. Thank them for protecting you and your loved ones.

I CAN

approach a firefighter or police officer next time I see her and

THANK HER FOR HER SERVICE

to protect me, my family and my community.

#49

I CAN

write local and national politicians to urge them to **SET TERM LIMITS FOR EVERY ELECTED OFFICE** in order to ensure fresh ideas and perspectives within government.

A politician who stays in office for more than two terms is like a family member who stays a month too long after Thanksgiving. One day too long is bad, but a whole month...

Many of us have seen a loved one wither away from a terrible disease or aliment. In 2009, Medicare alone paid more than $55 billion on the last two months of patients' lives.* Often, dying people go to intensive care units in hospitals to delay the inevitable. The average daily cost is $10,000 per day in ICU. We need to develop better ways for us to pass on with dignity and respect. – *CBS News, The Cost of Dying, 2010*

50

I CAN

make a healthcare directive that does not prolong my life artificially should my doctor believe my death is imminent. I Can do this with the **UNDERSTANDING THAT DEATH IS A NATURAL PART OF LIFE** and that resources used to keep me artificially alive only add to everyone's health insurance costs and is likely to place a financial burden on my loved ones.

#51

I CAN

embrace the idea that by living in America I have already been given more opportunity than most of the people who live on Earth; therefore, it is my duty to rely on myself and my community to support one another and reject assistance from the government should I be of able mind and body. I Can come to terms with the fact that NOBODY "OWES" ME ANYTHING but the freedom to pursue happiness.

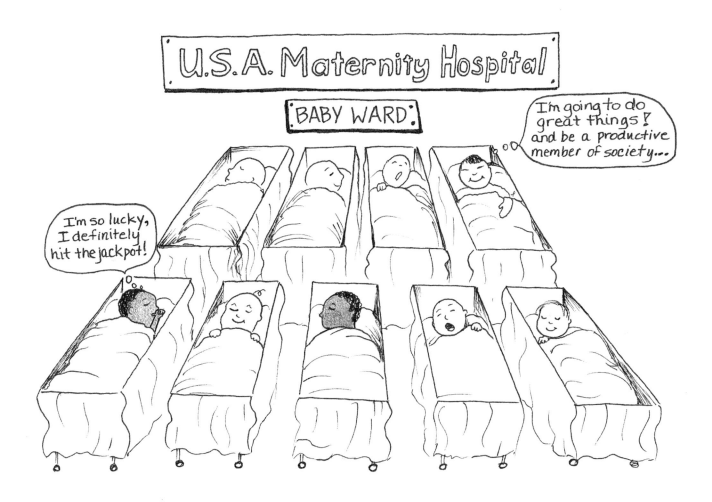

I think Warren Buffett said it best, that much of his success was due to the fact that he won the "ovarian lottery," referencing the fact that by simply being born in America he was given a huge advantage over almost everyone else in the world. Let's make sure future generations feel the same.

There are times in history in which generations are called upon to do great things. Most of the time it was a call to serve in the military to protect the nation from imminent attack on our freedoms and way of life. Today, those of us living now, have to take up the call to fix America ourselves without the help of government. Over the last 50 years we have been poor stewards of America and have made decisions that have jeopardized the long-term viability of a country that many died to defend. Now we must do what is right and fix the problems we face as they are real and serious. Inaction will have dire consequences.

I CAN

surrender to the fact that **I MUST ACTIVELY PARTICIPATE** to ensure that America remains the best place in the world to live for me, my children and grandchildren. I Can live my life knowing that history will judge my actions and commitment.

I CAN FIX AMERICA

MOSTLY TRUE STORIES

& OBSERVATIONS

It was a long time ago, but I want to share a story with you about how I chose the city where I was going to be born. In the spirit of full disclosure, before I decided where I was going to be born, I won this contest in the "choose your next adventure" series of the "Who Wants to Go to Earth" game show. I won top prize (it was a raffle, no skill involved. More on that later.). Behind the magic curtain was the grand prize: America as my birth-place. So already, before I took my first breath, I was already feeling kind of cocky. Whew, no Siberia for me.

Now the hard part: where to be born in America. I know, I know. How in the heck did I decide given all the wonderful places in America to live? I mean, California was just beautiful but, to me, it seemed a little bit too crowded. Everyone was being born there and I didn't feel like following "the cool kids." I considered being born in New York, but then I remembered that I would decide to go to college at Emory University in Atlanta and that by the time I arrived pretty much all my classmates would be from New York, so that didn't seem too adventurous. Texas seemed neat with all the land and the boots and the cheerleaders (yeah, I decided early on to be interested in women so I could move on to other important decisions in my life like who would be my favorite college football team). But then I remembered that Texas would always be there for me as a great place to visit with friends, do business, and maybe the best place to go if all hell broke loose.

So I did a little research guided by a few simple principles that represented the type of place I ultimately wanted to spend my first 18 years. These principles were:
- I wanted to find a place where hard work and innovation were rewarded. I wasn't expecting handouts; I was ready to work.
- I wanted there to be employment opportunities if I made the tough decisions to stay in school, constantly try to learn, and to work hard to be the best I could be.
- I wanted a safe place to live, grow and play in neighborhood. (I was a kid after all.)
- I wanted to experience all four seasons. I loved what I soon would call autumn.
- I wanted freedom to pursue my happiness, knowing that it was up to me to deliver results, be productive, and contribute to those who were truly in need.

GRAND PRIZE

You're going to be born in America!!!

Flint, MI

So through my research this Michigan town that piqued my interest kept popping up. This town's resumé was pretty strong: Birthplace of the world's largest company (General Motors), so there should be some innovation around. A vibrant middle class (good), generally safe neighborhoods (nice), and in a state that had water all around but also had snow in the winter for sledding. I liked to sled.

So it was to be: Flint, Michigan … ahhh, yeahhhh. Crack the bubbly (I mean bubble bath, I was a kid…dammit!).

And then whammo: I was born on November 1 in Flint. So far the plan was being executed beautifully, if I do say so myself.

All seemed good. Doctors seemed nice and gentle and had warm hands. Looked like I was born in a hospital instead of the back seat of a car, had two parents (although one looked a little old … could have been the lighting), and had a ride to a home after the party wound down, so that was cool.

As you know, there's not much to do the first few years except hang out, be fed, cry and soil myself. I guess in life not a lot of that changes … except the willingness of people to help you with the aforementioned items. Oh, FYI, it wasn't the lighting … the dude that was my dad, yeah, he was old. But he was cool and seemed to be a hard worker so hopefully I wouldn't have to crawl around trying to find a job. And just when I thought it couldn't get much better, I learned that my mom worked, was college educated, and had good health care. Cha-ching … fresh set of diapers every day. As far as I could tell, Flint was perfect. Wonder what my loser buddies were doing in California? Certainly not living it up like me.

As my glorious life of bliss and pampering continued, I did all the necessary things to make the parents proud: learned to speak, and of course gave the obligatory "mommy/daddy" mumbo jumbo just to make everyone happy. Then I learned to walk which was fun, but a little dangerous. Then I learned to read a little and tie my shoes, but then Velcro shoes came out around the same time so I was confused about this for a little bit, but I rallied and made it through, so all was good.

Then came the bike riding. Seemed unnatural at first. I mean, umm, the bike fell over all the time by itself, and you wanted me to be on it while this happened? No helmet, no problem thanks for the love. However, as I got on the bike I had my first encounter with magic: Apparently if you moved forward the wind or some magical wall or something held the bike up so you didn't fall. Pretty awesome that not only were my parents cool, had a home and worked hard, but that they were also wizards. My plan was progressing nicely.

Now that I could ride the bike I was off to learn how to swim in a big bathtub (I think they called it a pool). My dad thought it was important that I also learned how to hit a small white ball with a stick through the woods, so I amused him with his efforts to teach me. He called it golf; I called it crazy.

One day while I was out with my dad hunting for my white golf ball in the woods, he apparently forgot to put the garage door down when we left the house. It didn't seem like a big deal to me at the time, but after that day I learned that if you left your garage door open you were pretty much telling everyone that it was OK to come borrow whatever you wanted because it was free and we were through using it. Made sense. Dad must have forgotten that rule and, let me tell you, he was not happy about forgetting it. In fact, not only did people come by and think we were done using our lawnmower, but they also thought that since I wasn't riding my bike at the time, then I was probably through using my bike too. And the chain saw and the hedge trimmers. I was sure it was a simple mistake, and really it was my dad's fault for not following the universally accepted "Hey my garage is open go ahead and borrow what you want" rule.

But today, looking back on that experience, it was really the first time I thought, "Hey, wait, I don't remember getting a rule book of when it is OK for other people to take my stuff, but I will take this as an overlooked lesson I should have learned in my upbringing." Clearly, this was my and my dad's fault.

My dad had insurance, which meant that he paid some people some money in case he left his garage door up to replace the items in his garage. He also sold the same protection to other people who owned garages and garage doors, which could be left up accidentally. Seemed like a reasonable profession from my perspective, and I could see a lot of garages so the market opportunity looked large. Thankfully, the insurance company bought us all new things to put in our garage, and I was able to pick out a new bike so, all in all, it didn't work out that bad for me.

Then, something strange happened again. Dad and I were hanging out watching TV when the phone rang, and apparently my neighbor called and told my dad that there was another kid riding down the street on what appeared to be my bike. I was sure he just wanted to take that sweet machine for a quick ride, but my father didn't quite have the same outlook. "David, get in the car" was the clear and concise message delivered. No problemo as we both hopped up and got into my dad's car and drove up and down the streets to go visit with the kid who was riding my bike. Dad wasn't very talkative during our Sunday ride and was intent about visiting with the kid about how he liked riding my bike. Maybe the tire pressure was low, and dad was worried that the kid might get hurt, or maybe the chain needed grease. Regardless, Dad sure was worried about that kid riding my bike. And then, voilà, there was my bike with a kid on it who I had never seen before, riding the bike pretty darn fast out of our neighborhood. He must have been practicing for the upcoming summer bike race that I had heard all about. I was too young to enter but this kid seemed about the right age to compete. It was a nice day for a practice ride.

Once my father honed in on the kid riding my bike he told me to hold on. Now everyone knows that a car will always beat a bike in a race so I had no idea why my dad wanted to race this kid on my bike. But here was my dad racing this kid, and as we both neared a finish line I couldn't see, my father popped open his car door and knocked the kid, and my bike, to the ground. Not fair rules in racing, Daddy. Someone could have been hurt.

I guess my father was really impressed with how fast that boy could ride a bike because my father kept asking him his name and where he was from. Sure enough, this boy was not only fast on my bike, but he was also a fast runner. My father was not so fast on his feet so I guessed my father would have to catch up with him at the bike race the next week and ask him whatever questions he wanted to ask. My father sure was upset that he didn't get to talk to the boy. But my dad grabbed my bike, put it in his trunk, and drove back to the house upset and dismayed about how the neighborhood was "going to hell," or something like that. Not sure what that meant, but come to think of it, it was kind of weird that that young boy didn't just knock on the door to see if he could practice for the race with my bike. I would have let him ride it.

Again, not sure if I missed one of the rules of living in Flint, but it just seemed that if you wanted to ride someone else's bike you should have just asked. Easy as pie. And since I lived in one of the most innovative towns in America, based on my pre-birth research, it just seemed logical that one would simply have asked to borrow one's bike. Or made one yourself. There were factories all over this place.

As summer drew to a close, and autumn passed without any major excitement, one of the first winters in my memory came into focus. You may recall, I loved the four seasons and that was why Michigan was such a great place to be. So as that year's winter unfolded before me, my dad told me that I needed to go up into the attic to find what he called Christmas lights in order to light up the bushes outside, or something like that. Made no sense to me, but I pretty much had to do what he asked me to do. Begrudgingly, I went up into the freezing attic and started handing down boxes of tangled lights with colored light bulbs in them. Apparently I didn't do a good job of hiding my displeasure about this task as my father asked me, "What the heck is wrong with you, boy?" I told him it was freezing, and the boxes were heavy, and I wanted to drink hot chocolate and play with my Legos. It was at that moment I learned the true secret of Christmas lights. To this day I am not sure whether I am supposed to disclose this knowledge, but here is the equation as I learned it from my father: Christmas lights + bushes + ladder + danger = beacon and landing area for Santa and his sleigh of toys. At that point I was sold and could easily understand the need to quickly get the lights up and out. Dad and I were aligned with the mission.

So we began that frigid day just after Thanksgiving untangling lights and wrapping the bushes all over the place with our eyes on the prize: new toys. Of course, in the process of implementing Operation Santa Beacon we smashed, twisted off and broke a few of the colored light bulbs. At the end of the installation of lights my dad said that we needed to take a break and run up to Franks Nursery and Crafts to buy new light bulbs. Sounded good to me. The more the merrier, and maybe more lights equaled more presents!

We jumped into the car and headed out of the neighborhood toward Franks. It was snowing a little bit and the roads were getting slick so my father didn't drive too fast. As we exited the neighborhood, we passed two guys walking in the snow who seemed not to be really walking on the street but through yards and up driveways. I was sure they just wanted to play in the snow. As we drove by them, however, my dad said something to me that just seemed really odd with all the talk of toys and lights and Santa. He said to me, pointing at the guys: "David, do you see those guys there? They are up to no good." Up to no good? What the heck did that mean? Were they going to melt the snow? I didn't think they were going to borrow my bike because I saw the garage door go down, and no one raced bikes on the snow. That was just plain dangerous. That couldn't be what he was talking about, so I just let it go and we continued on to Franks to pick up a few lights bulbs to create one of the greatest Santa beacons on the street.

We drove back to the house about 20 minutes later and pulled into the driveway. As we pulled up to the house, we noticed that the lights on the bushes didn't seem to be as radiant or glorious as they once were. Maybe the falling snow covered up some of the lights. It made sense to me, but then again I was only about 8, so my knowledge of light waves, etc. was limited. My father seemed more alarmed and jumped out of the car and ran around the yard checking the lights. I could tell he was not happy. Maybe we didn't buy enough replacement bulbs and we would have to go back to the store. It was always a pain when that happened so I understood why he might be upset. He then uttered those now infamous words: "David, get back into the car."

Now we were in the car and driving a little faster than we had previously, despite the road and weather conditions. My dad drove up and down every street in the neighborhood looking for something. What he was looking for I had no idea, and he didn't feel like sharing that information with me at the time. Then he pointed and asked me, "David, are those the same guys that we passed earlier going up to Franks?"

I told him I thought so because honestly there weren't a lot of people walking around during a snowstorm. So my father pulled the car up to these two gentlemen in the pouring snow to ask them, I guess, some questions about lights, or decorating, or something. I heard him talk very politely to these men as they walked closer to my father and his car. It seemed like they were engaging in simple small talk when, out of nowhere, my father grabbed the arm of one of the gentlemen, twisted it behind him, and slammed the guy onto the hood of his car. My dad then said things that I could not repeat or really understand, but it was something about the man's mother and that it was wrong to steal. My father ripped open the jacket of the man on the hood of the car and, like a cat tangled in string, this man was wrapped from waist to neck in Christmas lights.

My dad made him give back all the lights, and then we went on our merry way. I guess these guys were worried Santa wasn't going to visit their house, thought that we had enough lights already, and maybe they could borrow some to make sure they were not overlooked by Santa. Made sense to me. But then again I was 8 years old.

But when I thought about it, it was a little weird that in a place as successful as Flint and with such a large working-class population, people wouldn't be able to pay for their own Christmas lights in order to flag down Santa and his toys. Those guys who took our lights must have been from another town where maybe they didn't have very many Christmas lights. I understood; not every town in America was the birthplace of the world's largest company. I knew it was OK to share. I just wished they would have asked for lights, not just have taken ours without asking. At 8 years old I knew that was rude behavior and I hoped those guys were grounded for a while.

As time passed and I got a little older, I noticed that as I rode the bus to school, more and more yards were not mowed and the houses looked like they could have used a good paint job. This was perplexing: Since Flint had all the basic infrastructure and track record for greatness, I wasn't sure why some select few people decided to make the place look less than stellar. Who knew — maybe they were too busy working making cars, and car parts, and other neat innovative things. Sometimes I worked so hard on my homework that I forgot to brush my teeth before I went to bed, so I knew that mistakes could happen.

But the yards never got mowed. The homes never got painted. The streets never got fixed. Apparently by then you didn't even have to leave your garage door open for strange people to come into your house and borrow whatever they wanted. In fact, a neighbor had people come into their house, and open up the garage, and then take the stuff in the garage. That violated the rules as I once understood them. Garage open = you can borrow my stuff. Garage shut = I'm about to use my stuff so please don't borrow it. What in the world did it mean when someone else,

without your permission, opened up the garage door and borrowed your stuff? Not sure, and it was confusing to me, but to top it all off there were rumors in the neighborhood that if you did leave the garage open and people borrowed your stuff actually no one was bringing these items back after they were through using them. Apparently the rules were changing and I was having a hard time figuring this out.

How could this happen in the thriving city of Flint, Michigan? I mean, every article I read prior to deciding where I would be born was about how great the city was, and how many jobs, and how safe … did something go wrong? Was I really not in Flint? This was really weird. I mean, the cars looked a little different than in the research I read before picking Flint. A little smaller, wider, a little more boxy. But hey, this was an innovative city, and a lot can change from 1964 to 1965.

… But then I saw a sign that said it was 1983. Based on my winning raffle grand prize I chose to be born in Flint in 1965, but based on my current math, I figured out that I was actually born in 1975. Um, hello, customer service department? I need to speak with a manager about fixing the error of my birth year.

Thanks. Sure, I'll hold for a little bit.

Of course, being able to choose when you are born, to whom you are born, and even more specifically where you are born is all just crazy talk. Yes, it is true, I was born in Flint, Michigan. Yes, it is true that things were stolen while I was growing up, and yes, it is true that my father was older when I was born (he was 52).

And equally true is the rapid decline of my once-great birthplace and my home state of Michigan. At one time, Flint was the place to be, to thrive, and to live the American dream. Today, Flint leads the nation as the most violent city in America and also has one of the highest rates of unemployment.

What concerns me the most, and the reason I feel compelled to write this book, is I feel as though I am living through my youth once again, but now on a national scale. I don't have the naïveté of being in grade school and high school watching this happen. I write this book with a few life lessons under my belt and with scars of being an entrepreneur who has had some failure and some success in business. I write this book as someone who feels and believes that people are generally good but that, as a nation, many of our economic and social issues have become so problematic that we feel helpless and scramble for any amount of security available, often neglecting our fellow American.

But how did we get to this place? And how did Flint go from being one of the best places to live in America to being ranked the worst place to live in America by Money Magazine? And really, all this in a course of 25 years. How the heck did it happen so quickly and what can we learn from it to make sure it doesn't happen as a nation?

One of my peers from Flint has made a name for himself by pointing out the downward spiral of Flint, and the companies and corporate decisions that led General Motors more or less to abandon the city and its workers. Michael Moore sees Flint in a different light than I do. He sees the workers as victims and General Motors and greed as the culprit. I respect and understand his point of view, and I cannot thank him enough for bringing Flint into the limelight as a case study from which we all can learn. But I want to take his message a little bit further and say that not only was it the fault of General Motors, but it was also the fault of the people of Flint. It was union leadership that fought assembly line efficiencies with output quotas and mandatory overtime. It was the people of General Motors and the union that didn't demand excellence in manufacturing, but instead squabbled about benefits and retirement perks while Japanese automakers kicked our butt.

But above all, in my opinion, it was the government policymakers that steered this country into a ditch with our ridiculous trade policies and incentive to outsource jobs to other countries.

Ever wonder why companies make stuff in places other than America these days? Well, get ready for the answer because you might not like it: That one is your fault. Yep. Really.

The first part of recovery is admitting you have a problem.

Our problem as Americans is that we want to have our cake and eat it too. For example:
- We want American jobs, but we also want the lowest price possible so we constantly buy products from foreign companies.
- We want security, but we won't make the tough decisions to become entirely energy independent.
- We want to be healthy today and enjoy a high quality of life as we age, yet we resist putting in the work to achieve those goals, and instead eat processed food and drug ourselves up with prescriptions that mask our health issues.

America, as we know it and have experienced for the past 50 years or so, is about to change. It will either progress from where we are today or it will decline, just like Flint did, at a rapid pace. At this stage, I am not optimistic about the future unless each of us commits to being better.

Our leaders do not lead anymore; they often only make the problems worse. And like herds of cattle, we seem to believe whatever these clowns say and elect them into office year after year. We feel good about this process because "they will fix it so I can go on living my life the way I want." In reality, however, the power that Americans have entrusted to our leaders has been mostly neglected and abused. Are we better off than we were 50 years ago as a nation? I think it would be hard to argue that we are, on almost every level.

So why do we continue to decline? In my opinion, it boils down to simple, time-tested truths that for some reason have become OK to violate. These laws of nature will last forever, long after you and I (and maybe even America) are gone. They are the "truths" that are missing from our national debate and our individual lives.

The violation of these principles eventually brings to a head massive and unpleasant change in order to restore balance to the universe and to nature. You can either believe this or not. But over time, certain principles are without debate. Simple things like:

- I cannot eat more calories than I burn and remain the same weight.
- I cannot spend more money than I make and be financially sound.
- I cannot be selfish and hope that people will help me in a time of need.

Yet for some reason, we have let companies, friends and even the government lead us down paths that violate many of these core principles.

How are we expected to preserve our right to pursue happiness as declared in the Constitution when, at almost every turn, we undermine the long-term viability of this nation and its people? I am not talking about just government policy but also the most important policy of all, the one that transcends all governments, religions and marketing campaigns, the policy that individually, we are accountable to ourselves and each other for our survival.

As an example, let's imagine a world in which government provides just the basic infrastructure and judicial and security systems in order for us to go about our lives in a safe environment. In this world (which doesn't exist right now), how would we behave; how would we operate our businesses; how would we participate within the communities in which we live? Would it be different from how it is today?

The problem, as I see it, is that we have "outsourced" many of our social and financial problems to the government. But have we ever stopped to think that perhaps the government isn't designed to handle many of our social and financial problems? Perhaps the reason we have allowed this system of entitlements and safety nets to exist is because we, as Americans, have been too lazy to take up the burden ourselves. Sure, it is easier to pay more taxes when the times are good, so you can "outsource" the responsibility of feeding the homeless, or providing housing for the poor or disabled. But what happens when the good times end and we have a locked-in cost structure that was based on a booming economy? Just look around. You are seeing exactly what happens right now, today.

But whose fault is it? It is mine, and it is yours. It is not just Washington or politicians or companies. All of the aforementioned are just groups filled with people. These groups have power and influence only because we have given them our power and influence. If we allowed our nation to be governed with a balanced budget would we have a debt crisis? But hey … times were good and the long-term consequences of violating the laws of living within our means were violated. Now we are paying the price.

American Citizen	
2011 Hunky Dory Lane	
Utopiaville, USA	Date: April 15, 2012
Pay to the	
Order of: US TREASURY	$ 100,000
One Hundred Thousand and xx/100	
Memo: 2011 Taxes–FIX EVERYTHING…Thnx!	

In the same way, we are paying the price by having our children's education be outsourced to the same government that cannot obey simple mathematical principles. We are so far deep into this dysfunctional cost structure and the "because that's the way it's always been" mentality that it is difficult to restructure to put the needs of the students above all the unions and special interest groups. That unsustainable mentality is one sad cop-out for parents who truly care about the long-term success of their children.

We get so hung up in America about the way things "used to be" or "have been" instead of obsessing over the things that need to be changed to make things "the right way." The right way to do things is a hard path to follow and is often not convenient or fun. But what it lacks in convenience, it makes up for in a sense of accomplishment and sustainability. I hate waking up in the morning to work out, and I don't manage to do it every day, but I know that the discipline it takes for me to get up will be paid back tenfold with how I feel and how productive I can be during the day. Not to mention all the health benefits. But is it fun? Hell no. I dread it. But it's part of the deal, part of being a living organism; it survives only by being healthy. Law of nature, pure and simple.

We, as Americans, have let the long-term viability of America be violated by a short-term window of perceived benefits. Sure, we can spend ourselves out of the depression in the 1930s; sure, we can fight two wars without having money to do so; sure, government can take care of everyone who doesn't have a job and still promote innovation and entrepreneurship. Yes, all these things work perfectly. Ummm, not quite.

I hate being a bearer of bad news but the time has passed, my friends, in fixing America through elections and campaigns. That path has failed us and will continue to do so. The only real change will happen when the masses, you and I, begin to be conscious of our decisions, choices and the way we are active within our community. Every day, every year, all the time, forever. It is truly the only way we can restore America.

And in that spirit, I have written this book. I am amazed that I find myself here writing these words when, in fact, most of you already know much of what I am saying. It is simply paying attention and doing the work where we often fall short.

In the past, our great leaders would focus on the things that brought us together, that made us all Americans; they would inspire us to lead, change and sacrifice. Today, our leaders stoke hatred, fear and misinformation in order to create a more divided and less powerful citizenry. Today, I want to suggest that you commit to follow some of the 52 items listed within this book. These are not perfect ideas, and some will resonate more than others, and you may flat out disagree with some, and that's OK. I believe that once you commit to participate in making America a better place by your actions, not your words, great things will happen. We don't have to agree on everything, but we do need to believe that together, with common purpose and simple common-sense solutions, we will be able to restore America to her greatness and preserve all of her positive attributes for the generations to come.

The world is watching each one of us. This moment in history will be judged as the time when Americans either got their act together and worked toward the common good or a time in which division and political games brought down the greatest country the world has ever known.

All I know is this: One day, near the end of my life, I want to look back and say I did everything I could think of to save our great country. I want you to feel the same way.

Now, enough talk. It's time to get to work. I believe I Can (and You Can) Fix America.

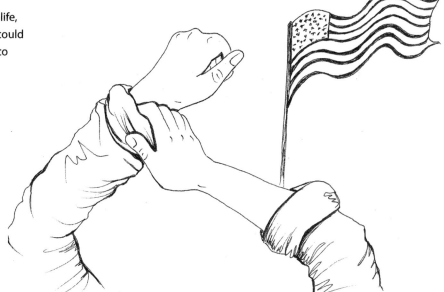

"And so, my fellow Americans:

ASK NOT WHAT YOUR COUNTRY CAN DO FOR YOU -

ASK WHAT YOU CAN DO FOR YOUR COUNTRY."

-JFK